Laughter Heard
from the Road

Maggie O'Dwyer

To Anne.

Laughter Heard
from the Road

*Best wishes Maggie x
M O'Dwyer.*

Templar Poetry

First Published 2009 by Templar Poetry
Templar Poetry is an imprint of Delamide & Bell

Fenelon House
Kingsbridge Terrace
58 Dale Road, Matlock, Derbyshire
DE4 3NB

www.templarpoetry.co.uk

ISBN 978-1-906285296

Typeset by Pliny
Graphics by Paloma Violet
Printed and bound in India

for Dorothy Molloy

Acknowledgements

Thanks are due to the editors of the following, in which some of these poems have appeared: *THE SHOp, Féile Filíochta, Piqué, Solitaire, Yes, I'd Love to Dance,* (Templar Poetry), *Thornfield - Poems by the Thornfield Poets,* (Salmon Poetry).

For their constant support and encouragement, my thanks to Gerry, Jane Weir, the members of Thornfield Poets, in particular, Ivy Bannister, Celia de Fréine, Louise C Callaghan, my family and friends and Alex McMillen. Special thanks also to Paula Meehan.

Contents

Passenger

No one will ever know
that other journey you drift into,
a passenger in a silent car.
The one where you glimpse
just what you might be capable of.

You hope not to be left there,
its fields wide and lonely as the sea.
Surely someone will take
the dagger from your hand,
lift you from the canopied bed
that billows and trails
down the river.

Memory

With your small hands
you lift the sculpted waves
of the ocean to your cheek –
smooth as an olive.
Water whispers in the cave
of your ear hollowed down
to low strings. You close
your eyes, listen to the heart
beat of the sea, a sound
you will remember when loss
gathers your breath and holds it.

Mantle

She weaves broad fields
of memory, a car journey
in twilight, where the long
blue-grey of her father's loss
follows the road home.

She weaves the patterns of love,
its soft scarred hills and desire
like the bitten absinthe flesh
of burgundy plums.

She weaves the house,
the textures of guilt,
her foot as it moves
beyond the boundary line
and, in between, mistakes
like slubs of silk, bleed
into her ordered rows.

Box

Say you have a box.
You paint it the colour
of a peacock's neck.
In this box you put
everything you've loved
and then you close it.

You have to close it,
don't you?

But some nights
you open it and crawl in.
You eat a Sunday salad
of scallions, tomato, ham,
half a boiled egg.

You put on her gold ring,
his Wolsey check shirt,
wrap yourself in the slatted light
of summer, sleep to the sound
of rain on cardboard,
in a heady mix of pomade,
face powder and gin.

Apple Tart

I kneel for your rosary,
bow my head as you pull
through my hair
a fine-tooth comb.
You're so neat I love you,
the thin frame of you
in the bed, me, between
you and the wall.

At night-time she grows
in the kitchen, like warm yeast
she flows out beyond the rim
of herself, falls into hay,
stacked like a beehive,
as his hand opens
the printed flowers
on her cotton dress.

I climb for your bell, bring
you bread soaked in milk,
your magic beads. I watch
you unpin your knot of silver
and lulled by the click and drone
of "She's so bold, so bold,"
I sleep.

Daytime, she slaps onto
the dusty table her soft mound,
rolls it flat as a harvest moon
seals the fruit with ribbons,
the print of her thumb.
The smell rises, sweet as apples in hay.
I purse my lips, afraid to eat it.

A Good Driver

Would he be proud watching me now
as I drive around in the rain, saturated
in the colours that I love.
Would he sit beside me in the car,
wait patiently as I run into Xtra-vision,
amuse the young men by saying,
"Anything with Clive Owen
or visually stunning will do."
Would he roll down the window,
rest his arm on the sill, turn his head
as I sprint into Superquinn for two bottles
of Evian and a packet of cigarettes.
Would we have a smoke, sit down low,
let the ash fall languorously on the floor,
watch the world?

It's Sunday in the suburbs
and not far from here there's a mist
stroking the top of a mountain, seeping
into the small hidden flowers of the bog.
We used to go there, didn't we – again and again,
up to Lough Dan, down through Sally Gap
and home through Roundwood?
He was proud of me then, the way I handled
the car, with the full load of us in it.
Kitty, Matt, Peter, Bill, Biddy and Margaret.
We never went for a walk, but we all piled out
to sit on a wall, have a cigarette and a long look
at the lake deep and dark beneath us.

I loved you then, I loved you all.
The warm comforting fogged-up place
we stayed in, the look of rain
its mossy edges drifting and blurred
your voices soft as bog cotton,
solid and clear as the gorse.

It's Sunday in the suburbs.
I put my seat belt on, drive to Homebase
for a bulb, on to Marks and Spencers,
down to level minus two and the sinister
edgy sound of rubber on rubber,
on into the frozen world of chickens
and dark chocolate.
"Would I like a plastic bag,
would I like cash back,
could I punch my number in?"
I'm out past the glasses, bed linen
and sofas, into the empty film light
of the car park.

He's very quiet, I notice.
I sit into his silence, happy now,
alone together in the car.

Pink Corset

You grew fat on silence
and the long shadow
of a cup.
The houses around you,
tight as elastic, marked
your soft skin.
You talked to strangers
on the bus,
stole tins of anchovies
and 60 watt bulbs from
the local shop.

When you took your
corset off, you felt like
you were falling
in an open field, so you
put it back on again;
and after one glass of wine,
pale as the last gaps
of light in trees,
you became the sound
of a clock, the long spin
of a washing machine.

Princess

Could it have been the way they cut
her hair, that primrose voile dress
with scattered pink roses, the soft kid
shoes, pale as the flesh of an avocado,
her delicate wrists and ankles, the silk
socks, her lips? Or was it the ornate chair
they sat her on, her legs dangling,
the sound of the shutter or that look
as he lifted the cloth, that let her know
she could wreak havoc in this world?

Three Times a Bridesmaid

Forget the smell of salad cream,
tomato ketchup, prawns, a damp
cocktail of red flock and brown,
a circle of sweat beginning.

Take the best man
away from the big band, past
the gaggle from the Ladies
and the mammy-daddy-cousin-aunty
-whiskey-cupboard row, outside,

under a mist of rain,
that fuzzes your perm, to the lift
of your turquoise dress
in a doorway.

Wallflowers

I was happy there
sex-less in paradise
until he came
with his tongue sharp
as a flick knife
and an apple, rosy-red.
"Taste it," he said.
Oh, I knew
what he was after,
so I gave it to yer man
instead.
He thought he had me then
but I wouldn't budge.
"Right," he said
slithering off.
"Right yourself," I said,
"and good riddance."
I could hear him
all through the night
muttering in the grass.
"I am king.
I am water.
I am fire.
I am falling skin."
I nodded off.
Next thing I know
I'm outside the gate
lured by the scent
of wallflowers.
Cunning bastard.

Apple

I want to take all his clothes off
here in this coffee shop, where
the young men are dressed in black
and one wears a sash of lavender
around his waist, moves to the sound
of cups and Jimmy Scott singing
Slave to Love.

I want to unbutton his warrior's raincoat,
silence his mobile phone, sink my face
into the winter belly of his skin.
I'm tempted by his strangeness
but I long for the familiar –

the smell and taste of apple
on your lips, the nape of your neck
soft as cat-fur, and your eyes like shells
in water cupped in my hands as a child
in the prelapsarian light of summer.

Verge

I don't remember if the sex was good
or bad. I only remember his smell,
and the hotel nylon sheets, pink as nerines,
the magpie dark I wanted to stay in,
and the midnight church bell, emptying
into the frost square of the town.

A Quiet Night in the Suburbs

Remember the night, me in the bed,
the sound of your stone on my window.

The stretch from the garage and then
your hands holding onto the ledge.

Mammy and Daddy asleep in the room
darkened with curtains, the prayer book

closed on the table, the Child of Prague
alone in the hall.

Remember the night outside, cold and lit
with amber, the winter cherry tree that bothered

the neighbours with its flurry of petals
and branches… All quiet now,

only me awake and flushed in my nightdress
as I open the window and pull you in,

the earthy smell of you close to my cheek,
your lovely breath still warm from her kisses.

Bloodline

I wanted to be like you, turn cartwheels
in O'Connell Street, wear a tie
around my neck with no shirt, spin a car
close to the edge, eat coleslaw with curry.

I wanted you to look at me, the way
I looked at the bloomed curve of a mango
or a pear tree, white as a wedding gown.
To feel me like moss under your hand.

You wanted something different, to find
everything you'd lost, and so each time
you came back, you lifted and turned me
over and over, like a stone in your hand.

Knot

If I had known then, the future of our touch,
the ghost of smells that brought me back

in summer, autumn, winter, spring, to keep
the ritual of desire alive, to be your Belladonna,

I would not have let you be the temperature
of my hand, that made the red fish curl, turn over,
never stay still,

or honoured myself with guilt, that ancient threat
of fire and whore, that kept the weave tight
and bound us together like shared blood,

and meanwhile never to surrender, never to lay
myself out, from beginning to end.

If I had known then that you would be
a constant shadow in my dreams,
I would have had you somewhere

in the open, a hay field, a paper-blue sky above us
with one small cloud, the sound of our laughter
heard from the road.

Mattress

When I think of you I think of frost,
not beautiful the way it can be,
laid out on the grass or settling in fields
outside the town.

I see it the way it was, caught outside
in the dark, in the sound of your footsteps
coming round the house, passing the window.

I hear it in the door that opened
into the empty light of the kitchen and on
into the sleeping sounds of the house.

I taste it still, in the cold air of your lips,
in that sweet edge of secrets and desire.

...you, out of my head

The time I think is right. Bare winter,
just before dark, with a little nacreous
light to cast the shadow of geranium
leaves onto the wall and tip the string
of red hot chillies from a lively crimson
to a deep bordeaux.

I have all the instruments I need
lined up in a row on the kitchen table;
they are made from thin cold steel.
My hands are steady,
better than a surgeon's, the hands
of a bomb disposal expert.

I pause, distracted by a blue tit swinging
on a fat ball and that cat, where can he be?
I almost hear my lilies opening
in their vase. I take a deep breath and see
a pale delicate vein of moist green
on a white petal, the mustard roots
of my hellebores still trapped in their pots.
I'm poised, ready, I cut...

Clothes need air

In memory of Dorothy Molloy

Before I met you, my head
was a washing machine. Words
tumbled and bumped like tennis shoes
in a pillow. I would pull on a cigarette,
and listen to the jittery silence between
the slow and fast spin.

The breath of winter was in there,
the violet space of twilight,
the tree-boned sky. I could smell gin
and the absent smell of vodka,
hear the metal-buttoned sound
of my heart.

You were out there in your cardie
and that plain raincoat, pockets
full of lip-red and saffron clothes pegs.
You clipped them into your hair,
threw them like knives in a circus,
conjured them over your head.

Oh, what a day it was, the day
I met you, clear as an autumn sky
with a bit of a breeze that lifted
the dazzle of clothes on your line,
and, oh, the sound of your voice
when you turned to me and said,
"Clothes need air."

Vanilla

This is the way you looked in the photograph:
you were leaving her and I snapped you
as if I were shooting you – that sound.
As you moved towards your car,
you must have wondered,
but you didn't look back.

In the photograph your car is almost silver,
the light low, soft and vague at the edges,
the buildings pink from the sky,
and the sky the colour of ice cream.

You're just a silhouette in your dark hat and coat.
You look like somebody's father going home.

Delphinium

So much is so beautiful: the dark weight
of yew, its berries hollowed
with poison, the pear tree in blossom,
that fine mist that almost hides forget-me-nots;
even me longing for you and you longing
for her, even her, when love has taken her dress
and changed it into the deepest blue
in a summer border.

First Defence

I have a bottle, plastic
with a nozzle that squirts
foam onto my hands.

I rub it in between
my fingers, into my palms.
The strong and weak lines
of my history.

I do it carefully, push
my mother's wedding ring up,
reach underneath,
find the hidden skin.

I do not like the smell
but it makes me feel safe
and at the same time
vulnerable and stupid.

She is Water

I knew when I saw her kneel
in front of your painting
in the middle of the New Year's
party, with all those bodies
around her, drinking and shouting,
the small room full of the smell
of Guinness, that I had lost.

She was so mysterious and still;
and she had this way with colour
and a way of signing off
with a thousand kisses.
She crept into me,
before I even knew she was there.

I found myself drinking Bancha tea,
slicing my carrots diagonally,
eating brown rice with chopsticks.
I stopped eating tomatoes,
started tying up my hair
with ribbons of magenta.

I learnt about Metal, Fire, Wood,
Earth and Water – and you and I –
we were Metal and Wood.
"Not good," she said, "not good."

It was only later I wanted to tear
off her hyacinth dress,
choke the soft voice that said:
"Friendship is better than love."

This is After You Left

All through the night
the tulips move towards
the lamp you left on,
they open out white
like paper bowls.

It's quiet the way it can be
on nights like this,
the walls have their shadows,
their strips of Venetian light.

The gilded mirror holds
its image of a painting:
the edge of a chintz chair,
a floating golden angel,
your written words.

Altar

I find myself still, in the company
of rain and the slow buttery dance
of candlelight. Outside the wind
is a sea longing
for a smooth flat shore.

You told me the waves offered
you a watch and once you found
a tiny white cross in stones.

I kiss the secret that made you,
your voice like snow falling
in a dark place.
I kneel in front of your lost altar
and open my hands for the small change
from angels' pockets.

Fugue

I know how to
get out of my house.
I know how to run
without moving.
The path I take
is always straight
with no people
and no cars.
I can run faster
than Speedy Gonzales,
I've got plastic wings
and in my pocket
a field of frost, rain drops
on Alchemilla mollis
and after all these years
you and I
in the bathroom mirror
practising how to kiss.

Still

I think I might die.
The sky is about
to bury me under
its weight of grey.
Rosie, our black cat,
flies around the garden,
rushes into the house,
bolts up the stairs.
I think she knows
something.

It's so quiet,
I can hear the shift
of a fig leaf.
You creak around
in the bed upstairs,
unaware
that I could be dead,
when you finally
come down.

If I were a hydrangea...

I would be more beautiful
dead than alive, my body
peeled back and faded
to the classical chalk tones
of Farrow and Ball.

I could sit in a vase
on the kitchen table, watch
you gaze at me for hours,
take photographs with
your digital camera.
Zoom in close to the bleached
burgundy of my skin.

You could carry me
in your smart card
to the computer, print me
in a book. Write words like:
Skin. Beautiful. Old.

A Gun Against the Wall

There are some secrets we keep
like sweets hidden in our pockets.

I remember when you told me yours.
The door was open and I could hear
the comforting shift of cows in the shed,
smell the damp wintry dark seep
into the yard.

It was the one cow that saved you
you said, her face in the window.

I remember the slow train journey home
through the midlands where all I could see
was the melting shapes of trees and fields
and finally myself.

I remember the steps I climbed,
the door I opened, the silent shape
of things in the hall.

I remember finding the apple you gave me
and how it brought me to the floor
where I ate it skin to core.

Portrait of a Lady

She loves the sound of her hem bustling on grass,
the colour of it like a magpie's wing
and the way shadows define the shapes of sunshine.

In the silent tyranny of the house she abandons herself
to the chiaroscuro of things.
Mirrors catch the satined green of her shoulder
against the deep brush-stroked blue of a wall.

He chips away, nuzzles her cheek, tingles her
with violence, blows softly on her lips
the small promised breath of a kiss.

She has learned to look behind him, to observe
the troubled light in the drawing room, how it spoons
itself on porcelain, embosses itself on yellow chairs,
catches the edge of things.

She dresses for herself now, anticipating like a lover
the sheen on her skirts of milky dawns.
She has become vain, wrapped in her own secrets,
pleached like a hedge.

I Hate How You Use Me

Call the sky paranoid, skulking
behind the clouds, the grass mad
with rain, the wisteria neurotic.
Call the robin a loser, waiting
for someone else to turn up
a worm, the fox a cretin,
for standing on the train tracks.
Call the hedgehog a fuck-wit
in the glare of a car, the sunflower
a slut, the peacock a poofter.
Call the evening light a cunt
for fading, Artemis a bimbo,
the moon a big fat moron,
the fallen apple, a failure.

Hunt

I am pink, a glorious gladiolus
spotted inside like a foxglove,

veins the colour of rhubarb,
fingers tipped with limes.

I am the lady of many frocks,
the green-eyed cat underskirt
of an Indian prince.

How could you possibly recognise me
in my heavenly world disguise.

You only knew me in broad daylight
or shadowed me in the strobe-lit dark.

Now, I wear velvet shoes with soles
soft as the inside of a broad bean pod.

I follow you, the way you followed me.
Tell me. How does it feel?

Safe Window

I cannot paint this lily, the virid lines that hold
it in the shape of a crown, or paint its skin taut
with life, pulsed and shaded pink with power.
Our black cat Rosie stretches on my words.
I lay my head down on her soft fur shoulder,
feel her small head on my arm.
We both sigh in the quiet hum of the kitchen
and watch, in the dark window to the garden,
the flickering light of war.

Night brushes the rooms with velvet. Dreams
shift as I pump the brake pedal in the car, see
the poppies that I planted in your garden grow
their petals thin as paper, seeped with the colour
of bruised flesh. I turn the pillow from hot
to cold, while in the kitchen, the lily unfolds
to a dawn milked with fog, its heart fluorescent
green, the white wall stained
with its cinnamon fall.

Wormwood

Outside in the long grass, circles
of dandelion yellow; inside
under the window the absinthe leaves
of courgette plants, in case of frost.
It can happen – you know, late in May
one night and everything changes.

Like the first time he saw her.
He said she reminded him of a colour,
pale and fragile as a song thrush's egg.
You couldn't speak, you just held his words
ruffling in your throat and sat there,
dark as a berry.

Wild Boar Stew

Angel has a smile that makes him long
to know what Angel knows.

Behind her eyes, pigs sleep by the side
of the road, their pink ears nestled
in the pale flowers of hellebores.

She cooks and serves, feeds him
wild boar stew, her chestnut tart.

He sleeps and wakes and sleeps
and dreams of Angel.

She knows his house is haunted
and so… she rubs him down with salt,
cuts off a piece of his hair,

takes him up through the Maquis air,
brings him to the villages of the dead.
"They have the best views," she says.

The Rabbits of Skomer

I could lie in your voice,
float in it, drift out to sea,
hang off your soft vowel
sounds, make a hammock
in between the way you
pronounce rabbit, ra-bet.
I could stretch myself out
in the bluebelled grass
of your island, watch puffins
strut around on their sturdy
feet, rabbits frolic without fear
of fox or dog, and let's be honest
even if you're small, fat and bald,
you can have me, just say it again,
ra-bet, my li-tel ra-bet.

Take the Sedative

I have the aconite under my tongue,
the arsenic and rescue remedy
in my bag. I'm lying on my side
with a rubber guard in my mouth.
Piece of cake, I think.
"Four minutes," he says. "Deep breath
going down... now."
When I felt it I knew
I should have taken the sedative,
the trolley, the bed, the cup of tea,
the slice of white toast, the pat
of butter and jam.

I'm still not the better of it,
when I see you downstairs in the cafeteria,
eating a sandwich.
"Jesus, that was quick," you say.
"Can you give me a lift back to work?"

That night you hand me a CD
you've compiled for me, songs to cheer me up.
Somewhere over the rainbow,
and the big rock candy mountain, where
there are cigarette trees and lemonade springs
and all the dogs have rubber teeth.
On the disc you've drawn a scope.
At the top you've written: "Let's see,"
and at the bottom, "Wow, it's lovely down here!"

Infuse

It is not only the way you disturb me,
clutter my bare surfaces, move my cup,
that I love,
or how you open my mouth
with something you've found,
or the way you drift in water.

It is not only the way you draw your line,
or trust my hands with your blood,
that I love.
It is the way you forget,
and how you let me remind you,
you've forgotten.

Rewind, Pause

A drop of water slips down the inside of a glass
and there's the sound of rain, but I can't see it.

The door to the garden is a mirror of all that's quiet,
including me and that strange purple watering can,

the only thing we bought in Ikea, driving up to Belfast
and back again, into a landscape violet and blurred,

the windscreen splattered with rain, the wet colours
of night… spreading.

I wanted to stay there, beside you in the car,
as you took photographs with your mobile phone,

and I watched Woody Allen's *Manhattan* on your iPod,
listened to Mariel Hemingway say,
"Not everybody gets corrupted."

It felt like the end of something that night –
sensual and tender. All of us trapped on the M50,
inching our way towards the flood.

Awake

The last time
you fell, you
fell into
the ocean,
past seagulls
elegant terns
and the fragile
heads
of bladder campion.
Before you split
the water
soft as moss,
you saw
a rock pool
blue shadowed
by your small
self, where once
you lived
in the crevices
of pink crabs
and periwinkles.

Running Place

Kafka would be proud of her,
Tarkovsky would grab his camera and follow
as she runs down each passageway,
opens every door.

He would love the echo of footsteps,
the urgent shadow on green walls,
her breathless search,
in every empty ward.

He would love the iron bed,
the billowing curtains, the sallow
dusty light, when finally she finds him,
only to have him taken from her,

again and again.

Kafka would be proud of her,
Tarkovsky would grab his camera and follow
as she runs down each passageway,
opens every door.

I won't let go even though...

I am tired of smoking, the constant
lift to my lips of rolled paper,
smoke held in my mouth and blown out
like a long sigh. I smoke, I long,
I long for a smoke.
Meanwhile, the dark window is a mirror
I see myself in, and you framed on the fridge
smiling at me in your apron
of merry-go-rounds.

In the night mirror I stab out my cigarette
in a small iron ashtray shaped like a heart.
I write away my ghosts, I do what I am told,
whisper your name, seal it in an envelope.
I sit and watch as the edge of absence
seeps through the paper and with my finger
I tear across the fold.

Cadence

My mouth is full of music
and voices that live inside me
like ghosts. They plead in Arabic,
lay out their graves in sand.
A choir of women shakes
the blossoms from a pear tree
and in harmony my mother
waves goodbye, my father
sits beside me on that long drive
through the mountains.

All I can do is open my mouth,
all I can hope for is that you hear me
and that somehow I can give you
the sound of a mist and forgiveness,
found in a line of trees at twilight.

Wake Up Margaret

"Ten seconds," you say.
I do not believe you.
I hold on to a wedge
of pigeon sky.
My mother's arms
around a stone cross.
A nurse's hand stroking
my head, your blue eyes.
I hear my name.